TO BE A STRONG MAN OF GOD

100 BIBLE VERSES FOR MEN

Patrick Wilcox (ThD)

FOREWARD

Men - we can handle anything, right? We are strong, resilient and always dedicated to our Godly purpose. We never waver in our faith or get discouraged.

Well, I have news for you. From my work as a Christian counselor I can tell you that in today's ever-changing world, men need spiritual guidance and encouragement more than ever.

Thankfully the Good Book is full of reassuring verses and timeless words of wisdom.

I have made the book you are holding now as a Christian companion for men. It features 100 Bible verses that stand out as particularly relevant for men today. Its portable size and quick nuggets of wisdom are designed for the modern, fast-paced age.

It is my sincere hope that you will keep it with you and flick through its pages regularly to gain insights and encouragement when you need it. I hope it helps you grow in faith as you seek God's wisdom in your life. Use it often to remind yourself of the type of man you should strive to be - and why.

I also hope you can share any messages you find particularly profound with your loved ones and other men who need it. You have my wholehearted permission to copy any part of this book and share it so that it may benefit others.

One last thing. This book has been self-published by me personally, as opposed to a large publishing company. A review by you on Amazon would go a huge way to helping it reach other men of faith. My deepest gratitude to you in advance for doing this.

Wishing you an inspirational life in the light.

Patrick Wilcox, ThD

100 BIBLE
QUOTES
FOR MEN

Taken from the King James Bible and the New King James Bible.

'Be watchful, stand firm in the faith, act like men, be strong.'

1 Corinthians 16:13

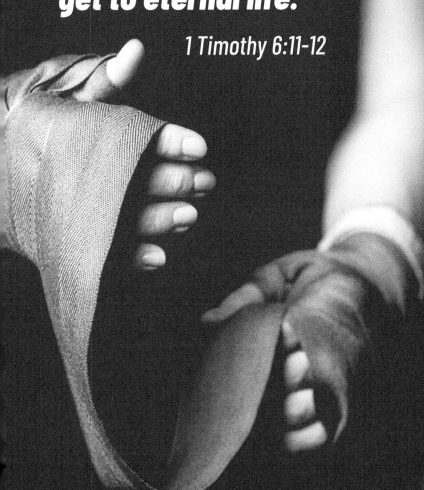

'God calls us to be fighters and fight the good fight of faith, where we may occasionally lose, but we should carry on until we get to eternal life.'

1 Timothy 6:11-12

'Iron sharpeneth iron, so a man sharpeneth the countenance of his friend.'

Proverbs 27:17

'But the Lord said, "Do not consider his appearance or his height. The Lord does not look at the things people look at. People look at the outward appearance, but the Lord looks at the heart".'

1 Samuel 16:7

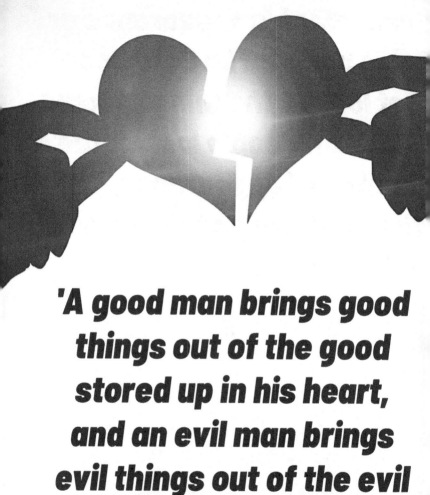

'A good man brings good things out of the good stored up in his heart, and an evil man brings evil things out of the evil stored up in his heart. For the mouth speaks what the heart is full of.'

Luke 6:45

'The steps of a good man are ordered by the Lord: and he delighteth in his way.'

Psalms 37:23

'Fathers, do not provoke your children to anger, but bring them up in the discipline and instruction of the Lord.'

Ephesians 6:4

'I desire then that in every place the men should pray, lifting holy hands without anger or quarreling.'

1 Timothy 2:8

'Husbands, live with your wives in an understanding way, showing honor to the woman.'

1 Peter 3:7

'Even the youths shall faint and be weary, and the young men shall utterly fall: But they that wait upon the Lord shall renew their strength; they shall mount up with wings as eagles.'

Isaiah 40:29-31

"What good will it be for someone to gain the whole world, yet forfeit their soul? Or what can anyone give in exchange for their soul?"

Matthew 16:26

'The father of a righteous child has great joy; a man who fathers a wise son rejoices in him.'

Proverbs 23:24

'You, therefore, have no excuse, you who pass judgment on someone else, for at whatever point you judge another, you are condemning yourself, because you who pass judgment do the same things.'

Romans 2:1

'Blessed is the man who walks not in the counsel of the wicked, but his delight is in the law of the Lord, and on his law he meditates day and night.'

Psalm 1:1-6

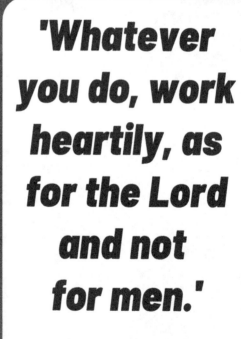

'Whatever you do, work heartily, as for the Lord and not for men.'

Colossians 3:23

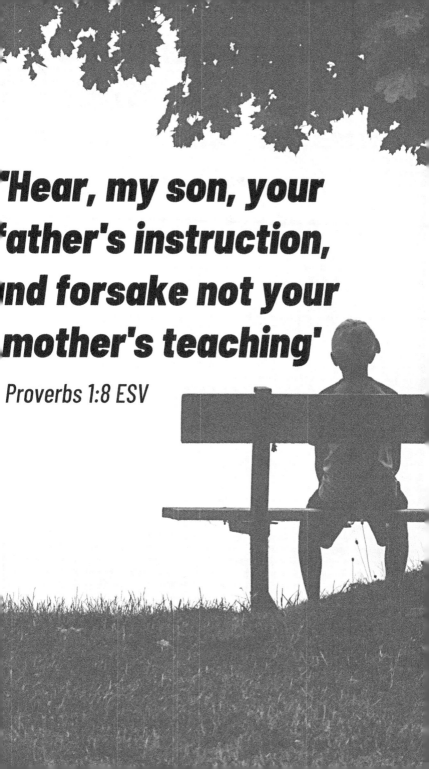

"Hear, my son, your father's instruction, and forsake not your mother's teaching"

Proverbs 1:8 ESV

'But if anyone does not provide for his relatives, and especially for members of his household, he has denied the faith and is worse than an unbeliever.'

1 Timothy 5:8

'Therefore, my beloved brothers, be steadfast, immovable, always abounding in the work of the Lord, knowing that in the Lord your labor is not in vain.'

1 Corinthians 15:58

'If you do wrong, be afraid, for he does not bear the sword in vain. For he is the servant of God, an avenger who carries out God's wrath on the wrongdoer'

Romans 13:4

'God created the heavens and the earth. The earth was without form and void, and darkness was over the face of the deep. And God said, "Let there be light," and there was light. And God saw that the light was good.'

Genesis 1:1-31

'If anyone thinks that he is a prophet, or spiritual, he should acknowledge that the things I am writing to you are a command of the Lord.'

1 Corinthians 14:37

'And God said to them, "Be fruitful and multiply and fill the earth and subdue it and have dominion over the fish of the sea and over the birds of the heavens".'

Genesis 1:28

'But as for you, teach what accords with sound doctrine.'

Titus 2:1

'Because you did not serve the Lord your God with joyfulness and gladness of heart, therefore you shall serve your enemies whom the Lord will send against you, in hunger and thirst, in nakedness, and lacking everything. And he will put a yoke of iron on your neck until he has destroyed you.'

Deuteronomy 28:47-48

'Blessed is the one who perseveres under trial because, having stood the test, that person will receive the crown of life that the Lord has promised to those who love him.'

James 1:12

'Be not wise in your own eyes. Fear the Lord, and turn away from evil.'

Proverbs 3:7-8

'And if it is evil in your eyes to serve the Lord, choose this day whom you will serve, whether the gods your fathers served in the region beyond the River, or the gods of the Amorites in whose land you dwell. But as for me and my house, we will serve the Lord.'

Joshua 24:15

'But because of the temptation to sexual immorality, each man should have his own wife and each woman her own husband.'

1 Corinthians 7:1-40

'Be imitators of God, as beloved children. And walk in love, as Christ loved us and gave himself up for us.'

Ephesians 5:1-33

'You did not choose me, but I chose you and appointed you that you should go and bear fruit and that your fruit should abide, so that whatever you ask the Father in my name, he may give it to you.'

John 15:16

'So do not fear, for I am with you; do not be dismayed, for I am your God. I will strengthen you and help you; I will uphold you with my righteous right hand.'

Isaiah 41:10

"That the man of God may be competent, equipped for every good work.'

Ephesians 5:23

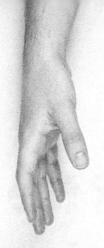

'Then the Lord God said, "It is not good that the man should be alone; I will make him a helper fit for him".'

Genesis 2:18

'Train up a child in the way he should go; even when he is old he will not depart from it.'

Proverbs 22:6 ESV

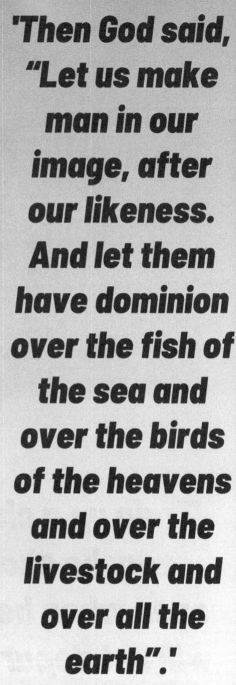

'Then God said, "Let us make man in our image, after our likeness. And let them have dominion over the fish of the sea and over the birds of the heavens and over the livestock and over all the earth".'

Genesis 1:26-27

'Then the Lord God formed the man of dust from the ground and breathed into his nostrils the breath of life, and the man became a living creature.'

Genesis 2:7

'For even when we were with you, we would give you this command: If anyone is not willing to work, let him not eat.'

2 Thessalonians 3:10

'If you love me, you will keep my commandments.'

John 14:15

'And God spoke all these words, saying, "I am the Lord your God, who brought you out of the land of Egypt, out of the house of slavery. You shall have no other gods before me".'

Exodus 20:1-26

'Moreover, he must be well thought of by outsiders, so that he may not fall into disgrace, into a snare of the devil.'

1 Timothy 3:7

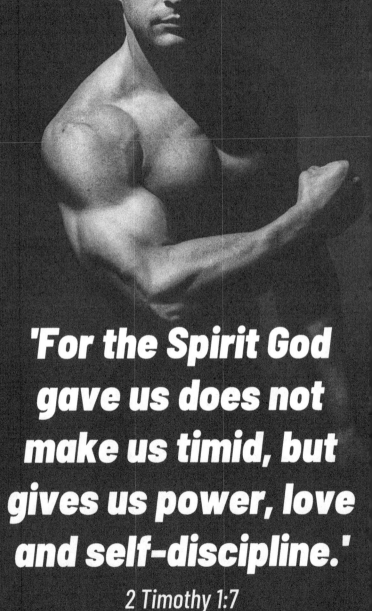

'For the Spirit God gave us does not make us timid, but gives us power, love and self-discipline.'

2 Timothy 1:7

'Husbands, love your wives, as Christ loved the church and gave himself up for her, that he might sanctify her, having cleansed her by the washing of water with the word.'

Ephesians 5:25-33

'But God shows his love for us in that while we were still sinners, Christ died for us.'

Romans 5:8

'Husbands, love your wives, and do not be harsh with them.'

Colossians 3:18-19

'But the fruit of the Spirit is love, joy, peace, patience, kindness, goodness, faithfulness, gentleness, self-control; against such things there is no law.'

Galatians 5:22-23

'Then the Lord said, "My Spirit shall not abide in man forever, for he is flesh: his days shall be 120 years".'

Genesis 6:1-22

'I urge that supplications, prayers, intercessions, and thanksgivings be made for all people, that we may lead a peaceful and quiet life, godly and dignified in every way.'

1 Timothy 2:1-15

'Honor your father and mother, that it may go well with you and that you may live long in the land.'

Ephesians 6:2-3

'And I sought for a man among them who should build up the wall and stand in the breach before me for the land, that I should not destroy it.'

Ezekiel 22:30

'For God is not a God of confusion but of peace.'

1 Corinthians 14:33-35

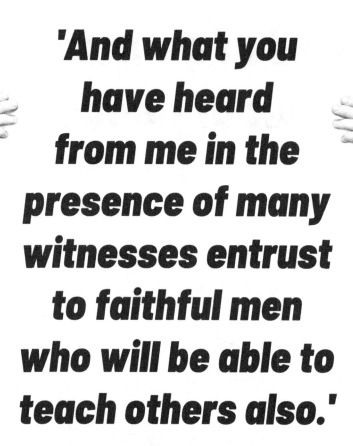

'And what you have heard from me in the presence of many witnesses entrust to faithful men who will be able to teach others also.'

2 Timothy 2:2

'And how from childhood you have been acquainted with the sacred writings, which are able to make you wise for salvation through faith in Christ Jesus.'

2 Timothy 3:15

'Our gospel came to you not only in word, but also in power and in the Holy Spirit and with full conviction.'

1 Thessalonians 1:1-10

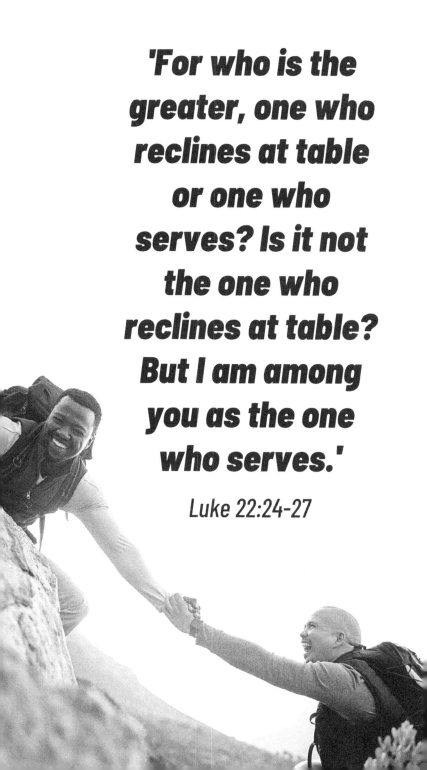

'For who is the greater, one who reclines at table or one who serves? Is it not the one who reclines at table? But I am among you as the one who serves.'

Luke 22:24-27

'Let the words of my mouth and the meditation of my heart be acceptable in your sight, O Lord, my rock and my redeemer.'

Psalm 19:14

'For God so loved the world, that he gave his only Son, that whoever believes in him should not perish but have eternal life.'

John 3:16-17

'The wicked flee though no one pursues, but the righteous are as bold as a lion.'

Proverbs 28:1

'There is neither Jew nor Greek, there is neither slave nor free, there is no male and female, for you are all one in Christ Jesus.'

Galatians 3:28

'Be strong and courageous, and do the work. Do not be afraid or discouraged, for the Lord God, my God, is with you.'

1 Chronicles 28:20

"Therefore a man shall leave his father and his mother and hold fast to his wife, and they shall become one flesh.'

Genesis 2:24

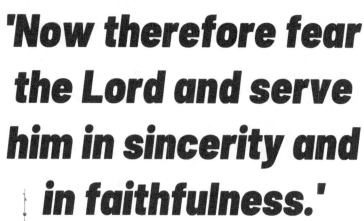

'Now therefore fear the Lord and serve him in sincerity and in faithfulness.'

Joshua 24:14-15

'And if you faithfully obey the voice of the Lord your God, being careful to do all his commandments that I command you today, the Lord your God will set you high above all the nations of the earth.'

Deuteronomy 28:1-68

'If you obey the voice of the Lord your God. Blessed shall you be in the city, and blessed shall you be in the field.'

Deuteronomy 28:1-68

'The Lord
God took
the man
and put
him in the
garden of
Eden to
work it and
keep it.'

Genesis 2:15

'An overseer must be above reproach, the husband of one wife, sober-minded, self-controlled, respectable, hospitable, able to teach.'

1 Timothy 3:2

'To the woman he said, "I will surely multiply your pain in childbearing; in pain you shall bring forth children. Your desire shall be for your husband".'

Genesis 3:16

'So God created man in his own image, in the image of God he created him; male and female he created them.'

Genesis 1:27

'Let each one of you love his wife as himself, and let the wife see that she respects her husband.'

Ephesians 5:33

'For I have chosen him, that he may command his children and his household after him to keep the way of the Lord by doing righteousness and justice.'

Genesis 18:19

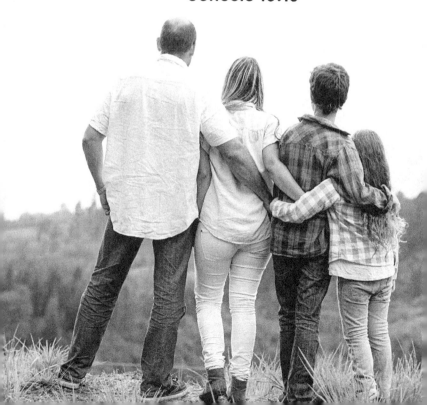

'For everything that was written in the past was written to teach us, so that through the endurance taught in the Scriptures and the encouragement they provide we might have hope.'

Romans 15:4

'Like a muddied spring or a polluted fountain is a righteous man who gives way before the wicked.'

Proverbs 25:26

'Fathers, do not provoke your children, lest they become discouraged.'

Colossians 3:21

'So God blessed the seventh day and made it holy, because on it God rested from all his work that he had done in creation.'

Genesis 2:1-25

'Be clothed with humility: for God resisteth the proud, and giveth grace to the humble.'

Peter 5:5

'Bodily exercise profiteth little: but godliness is profitable unto all things, having promise of the life that now is, and of that which is to come.'

Timothy 4:8

'Be stedfast, unmoveable, always abounding in the work of the Lord, forasmuch as ye know that your labour is not in vain in the Lord.'

Corinthians 15:58

'Man doth not live by bread only, but by every word that proceedeth out of the mouth of the Lord doth man live.'

Deuteronomy 8:3

'For the word of God is quick, and powerful, and sharper than any two-edged sword, piercing even to the dividing asunder of soul and spirit.'

Hebrews 4:12

'Confess your faults one to another, and pray one for another, that ye may be healed.'

James 5:16

'The just man walketh in his integrity: his children are blessed after him.'

Proverbs 20:7

'A wise man is strong; yea, a man of knowledge increaseth strength.'

Proverbs 24:5-6

'God is faithful, who will not suffer you to be tempted above that you are able; but will with the temptation also make a way to escape.'

1 Corinthians 10:12-13

'And let us consider
one another to
provoke unto love
and to good works.'

Hebrews 10:24-25

'Let every man be swift to hear, slow to speak, slow to wrath. For the wrath of man worketh not the righteousness of God.'

James 1:19-20

'O man of God, flee these things; and follow after righteousness, godliness, faith, love, patience, meekness.'

1 Timothy 6:11-12

'Be sober, be vigilant; because your adversary the devil, as a roaring lion, walketh about, seeking whom he may devour.'

1 Peter 5:8-9

'Blessed is the man that walketh not in the counsel of the ungodly, nor standeth in the way of sinners, nor sitteth in the seat of the scornful. But his delight is in the law of the Lord.'

Psalms 1:1-3

'The Lord is on my side; I will not fear: what can man do unto me? The Lord taketh my part with them that help me: therefore shall I see my desire upon them that hate me. It is better to trust in the Lord than to put confidence in man.'

Psalms 118:6-8

'Be strong and of a good courage, fear not, nor be afraid of them: for the Lord thy God, he it is that doth go with thee; he will not fail thee, nor forsake thee.'

Deuteronomy 31:6

'Rise up; this matter is in your hands. We will support you, so take courage and do it.'

Ezra 10:4

'God is our refuge and strength,
a very present help in trouble.
Therefore will not we fear,
though the earth be removed, and
though the mountains be carried
into the midst of the sea; Though
the waters thereof roar and be
troubled, though the mountains
shake with the swelling thereof.'

Psalms 46:1-3

'You who are younger, submit yourselves to your elders. All of you, clothe yourselves with humility toward one another.'

1 Peter 5:5

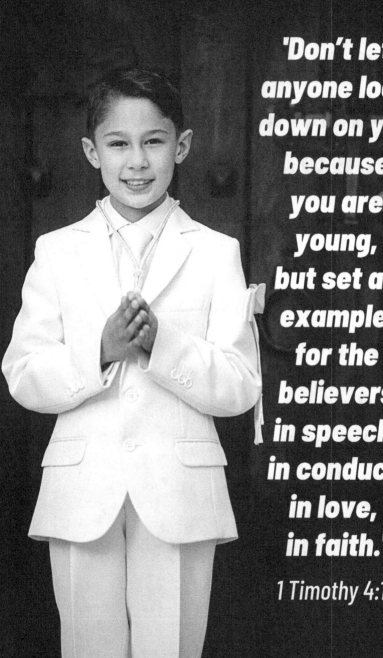

'Don't let anyone look down on you because you are young, but set an example for the believers in speech, in conduct, in love, in faith.'

1 Timothy 4:12

'Am I now trying to win the approval of human beings, or of God? Or am I trying to please people? If I were still trying to please people, I would not be a servant of Christ.'

Galatians 1:10

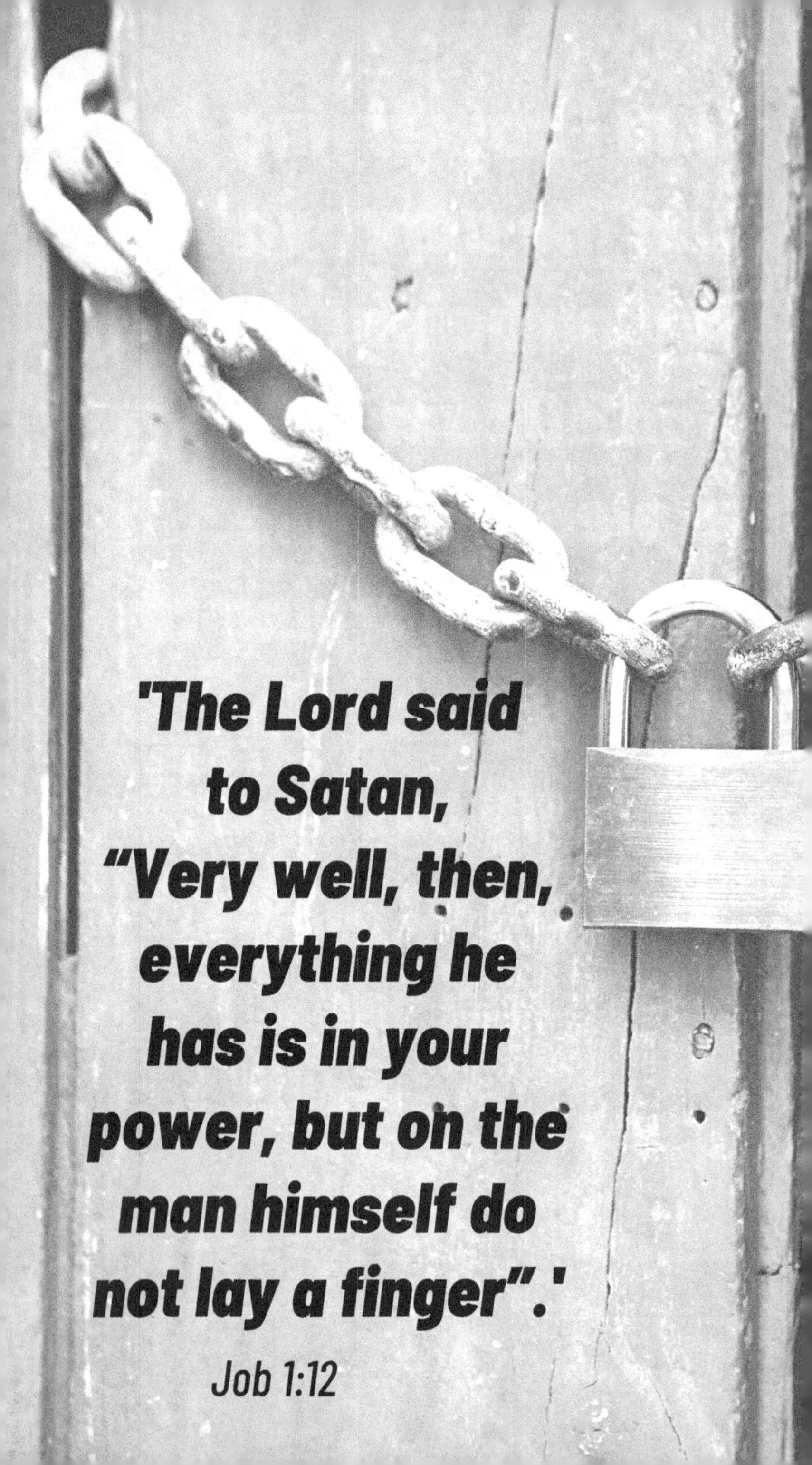

'The Lord said
to Satan,
"Very well, then,
everything he
has is in your
power, but on the
man himself do
not lay a finger".'

Job 1:12

'Fools give full vent
to their rage,
but the wise bring
calm in the end'

Proverbs 29:11

'How can a young person stay on the path of purity? By living according to your word.'

Psalm 119:9

'Good will come
to those who are
generous and lend
freely, who conduct
their affairs
with justice.'

Psalm 112:5

'Therefore we do not lose heart. Though outwardly we are wasting away, yet inwardly we are being renewed day by day.'

2 Corinthians 4:16

'One who has unreliable friends soon comes to ruin, but there is a friend who sticks closer than a brother.'

Proverbs 18:24

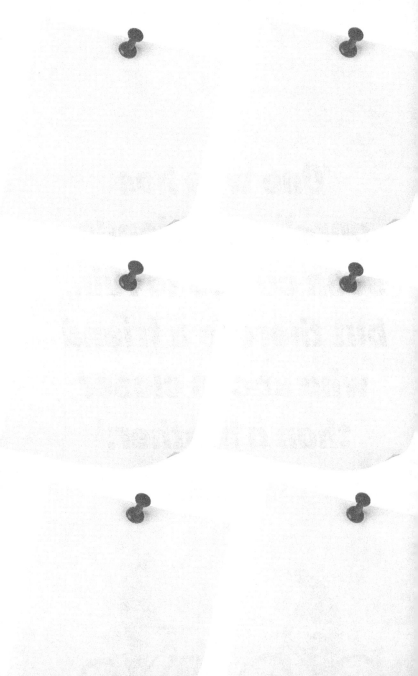

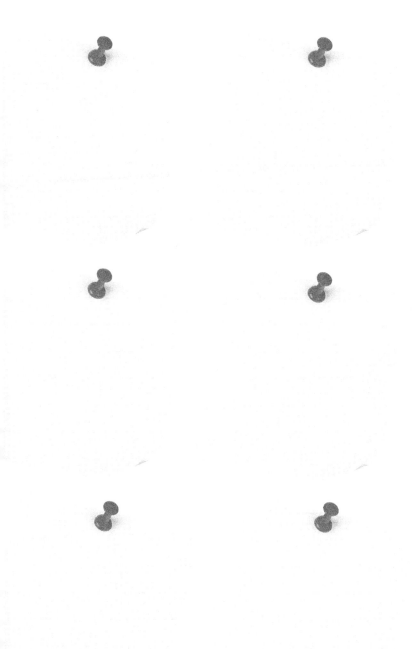

MY NOTES / THOUGHTS

MY NOTES / THOUGHTS

Made in the USA
Las Vegas, NV
23 October 2023